Praise for *Fenestration*

Othuke Umukoro's *Fenestration* is keenly aware of the violent implications of its title, but its sense of language and metaphor as repositories of historical complexity are broader than that. *Fenestration* carefully builds, arranges and peers through an array of portals: childhood memory of abundance and loss, collective memory of suffering and resilience, the dailiness of social life as a diasporic writer wrestling with poetic inheritance and possibility. Stitching his own transatlantic crossings—physical and psychic—through a harrowing imagination of the Middle Passage, Umukoro blends lush lyricism with observational directness, gazing with steady eyes at the world of fact and sensation and at the "coffined dark" within. Umukoro's is a bracing, painful and ultimately affirming vision: "Whichever way I look, I am what is bent."

—**MARK LEVINE**, author of *Sound Fury*

Othuke's heart-centric new work, *Fenestration*, is filled with tender poems of discovery. They stay with the reader long after the end of a page, and the book. The strength of these poems is in the refined delicacy of understanding, through dilated pupils, the bayonets' knife's edge. Both through the intimacy of complex love between father and son, and the sweeping and intimate pain of those Africans whose involuntarily journeys created the African diaspora we know today, we comprehend what it means to perceive the world through haunted, multi-century somatic knowing.

—**TRACIE MORRIS**, author of *human/nature poems*

Fenestration

Fenestration

Poems

Othuke Umukoro

WINNER OF THE 2024 X. J. KENNEDY POETRY PRIZE
Selected by Diane Seuss

TRP: THE UNIVERSITY PRESS OF SHSU
HUNTSVILLE, TEXAS 77341

Library of Congress Cataloging-in-Publication Data

Names: Umukoro, Othuke, 1990- author.
Title: Fenestration : poems / Othuke Umukoro.
Identifiers: LCCN 2025018798 (print) | LCCN 2025018799 (ebook) | ISBN 9781680034448 (trade paperback) | ISBN 9781680034455 (ebook)
Subjects: LCSH: African diaspora--Poetry. | Africa, West--Social life and customs--Poetry. | LCGFT: Poetry.
Classification: LCC PR9387.9.U484 F46 2025 (print) | LCC PR9387.9.U484 (ebook) | DDC 821/.92--dc23/eng/20250615
LC record available at https://lccn.loc.gov/2025018798
LC ebook record available at https://lccn.loc.gov/2025018799

FIRST EDITION

Cover art by Mercedes Rancaño Otero | istockphoto
Author photo by Joshua Thermidor

Cover design by Cody Gates, Happenstance Type-O-Rama
Interior design by Maureen Forys, Happenstance Type-O-Rama

Printed and bound in the United States of America
First Edition Copyright: 2025

TRP: The University Press of SHSU
Huntsville, Texas 77341
texasreviewpress.org

Contents

Fenestration

Mass

What was I thinking about
on my way here? passing
the small kenkey with rabbit stew joint, passing
Elmina Fishing Harbour, where
I stood yesterday watching
as Fante fishermen mend nets—
acid cry of pied crows.
It goes on for miles. This scarred heaviness.
Above, bitumen letters
on wooden slab, FEMALE SLAVE DUNGEONS.
I am the last to enter. Shoeless.
The walls of this one have patches
the colour of stale turtle tank water.
The size is a bullet.
When Emmanuel, our tour guide,
lanky fellow with keen eyes,
says nearly 150 of them were crammed here every month,
the man with short dreads is the first to break. Someone,
not the middle-aged lady
whose name in Shona means *give thanks*,
not the man whose hands remind me of garden urns,
someone digs for words
but finds a lint-free tissue instead.
The air pales.
I imagine gaunt bodies. The coffined dark.
I touch the walls. Then again.
Whichever way I look, I am what is bent.

Prologue

Because it
is not February, we are on our knees
gardening, & you are telling me otters
hold
hands when they fall asleep
so they don't drift apart.
"I did not know," I say.
"Now you do," you reply with a smile. Your eyes
the colour of molasses syrup.
All around us, dislodged
weeds, birdsongs, the raw of earth.
You're wearing that hat
you wore Friday morning when
we passed a bald
man wrangling with another bald
man for calling him bald
at the motor park.

Weeks after the second
miscarriage an antelope stood in
the yard, brown face towards
the window, quiet like pondwater.
You fed it— soft shoots, shrubs—every night.
Six nights? & then it was gone,
rustling into slivers
of moonlight.

What is memory if not commitment?
These dark clods.

Grit

Like everyone
else standing on this side of the ruin,
I watch as our Akan guide tries
to lift the cannonball and fails.
I imagine the castle's governor
with his Edam-cheese face looking
at us from up there, the balcony
that leads right into his residence,
where he stands and selects
as if in a store,
except it is not us he is looking
at but one of the enslaved women
in Elmina Castle
who has refused him,
who is kneeling, legs shackled,
raised hands carrying a cannonball.
The soldiers laughing, cussing
at her in a language so different
from her Ibibio.
But these soldiers, these
white-hot blades,
even the governor, know nothing
they do can whittle her—something
about the way
she sets her face, that birthmark
on her neck that looks
like the curving horn
of a Cape buffalo.
I imagine days later,
to serve as an example to the rest in
dungeons, they bind her to the cannonball,
still unbowed, as is often the case,

and hurl her into the ocean's jaws.
And when I say the ocean
is our largest unmarked grave,
what splinters
inside me splinters
inside me because it splinters

The Year My Father Died

Everything is in bloom.
Is this not how the body comes to the underground
language of silence—bliss, then reticent ash?
Somewhere in my life's wilderness, a village weaver prods.
Even now your head, scalp stiffened
from years of carrying spiky bunches of palm fruit
so your younger brother could afford technical school.
Even now your eyes. How you always mean everything
you did not say. Once, nine & a half, I thought malaria would
cull me until you raced, machete in hand, into the rainforest
& came back with root & bark that kept my frail body
from shattering. Did I thank you afterwards or fall asleep?
There is this seedless cry. The fungus green
of this month, my father, how could it mean *go*?

Poem of the Day

The only thing
about the man sitting on the tanned
bench some yards from mine is this:
his dog looks like a KGB agent.
Five ducks are on the river.
Behind the river is a sushi shop.
Behind the sushi shop, the motel
that charges a cleaning fee
but I'm the one who does the cleaning
& takes out the trash. Behind the motel,
nothing. I can't help
it. The walls are super thin.
The young couple
next room smoke pot, fuck, & talk
the same thing—vegan meatballs.
Sometimes I cover
my ears with pillows, but I still hear them—

For Pete's sake, who honks like penguins
when they're fucking?
The ducks are now seven.
I watch them dip their heads.
Beat buff wings. Dip.
In Confucianism, seven is harmony.
Who cried into my shoulder during recess
that July afternoon—almost seven, her father leaving
them for another woman?
I look into my journal. Riffle. All that talk
about the best way
to end a poem. I don't.
Care.

Thrust

The ground is red
& the sun is ironclad—
this is how I know I have arrived
in Salaga.
Inside the tro tro
the fellow beside me
is dozing off again.
When I descend at the dusty
WELCOME TO SALAGA SLAVE MARKET
sign, the time machine that is grief
porcupines——
On weathered legs
from kingdoms
that fasten.
A lad falters
& the whip claws
flesh pieces.
This woman is calling
the names of her children
or siblings or children
or friends or children
or lovers or children.
Isn't the tongue
the body's first talisman.
Look, this man
they're haggling
over has my father's firm chest.
Somewhere vultures' grunts
hew & I think flea-roads
to Sandema, to Assin Manso,
to grey.
I want to say something

but what—there is only this
fading into
where the word
of the day burns.

Waiting

Not the rose
carpet, not the steady breath of the ceiling fan
but the patch of sunlight squeezing through.
You've been here before.
You're early. Unlike

last time—stuck
in traffic. The other
passengers in the Keke Napep
did what people stuck in traffic do: smile
at strangers, tell the driver to change the radio station,
crack knuckles, complain, fall asleep,
wake & eat the agbalumos probably meant for the kids.
Then complain
some more. Everybody complains
but nobody is tired enough to dump this city.
Remember the acorn-eyed woman
who said politicians are Satan's assistants on earth?
& who was it that farted when traffic finally cleared?

When the doctor tells you
you're HIV positive,
you look from his young face to the mug
placed upside down on the table.
Concave base, azure handle
on a white body. It looks
like the one
your last boyfriend gave you.
...there are drugs
that can keep things under control...
A tear is a close friend. There is another
appointment. You rise.

It's almost June.
You walk down the dusty
street in the burning
the burning sun.

Ecdysis

Months after your father died
his brothers called for a meeting.
Alligator pepper. Kolanuts.
Palmwine. Garden eggs.
They wanted your mother
to marry his elder brother.
Her eyes shot arrows
at them. When they couldn't crush
her, they took
the piece of land. The herd of goats.
The house.

She moved
to the city with you, building afresh
from tailoring & selling avocados.
We've been walking for hours,
& you've stopped talking.
Marble berries. Wild mushrooms.
Twigs in sunlight.
We are where a curtained doorway
in the forest opens to a lake.
You offer a photo
of her from your backpack
& I do what eyes do
when they meet grace—
worship.

The Year Before the Year Before the Year Before the Year My Father Died

I am kneeling. Hands in the air.
Plods of sweat stand
like foot soldiers on my upper lip.
In the parlour that smells
of baby powder, he is sitting
on his favourite chair.
"So, you have decided
to be stubborn," he says fishing
for another garden
egg from the bowl.
I watch as he bites
into its smooth green skin.
"Did I stutter
when I said never you
go swim in that river
again?" he asks.
"Now, here is what I want you
to do. I want you to go
outside. Look for a cane,
one good enough for your type
of stubbornness."
Then he turns
away, chewing quietly.
I stand &
walk into the night.

I know where to find a good cane. I know I am not going there. I will just walk around & keep walking until the world falls asleep. I must have been walking for about an hour when I heard it. Light footsteps. I turn—tall tar figure in scraggy clothes. Even in coagulated darkness, Loco, the village madman, stands unmistakable. Long tangled hair the colour of boneless baked pork ribs. Should I run? Everyone knows madmen are better runners. He lays down the grubby bag slung over his shoulder, eyes never leaving me, & motions for me to sit. Villagers say he was a gifted young man until his jealous witch stepmother turned him into what he is now. Do you know why the husband is the one who sleeps on the side of the bed closest to the door? Loco asks. I shake my head. He looks at me the way a teacher would look at a nincompoop. So when robbers barge in he is the first to receive a blow to the head! Now your turn. Turn for what? I gasp. To ask me a question, he beams. I heave. Is what they say about your stepmother true? Where is your real mother? So many questions I want to ask. My stomach grumbles then, so instead, I ask: what will you eat for dinner? Sleep! What? I will eat sleep for dinner, he thunders. & with one swift movement stands & places the bag on his head. I will eat sleep for dinner, he howls. I will eat sleep for dinner. I will eat sleep for dinner. I watch him until the night swallows him, voice still rumbling in the distance.

I slip in through
the back
door, stealthy
as a jaguar.
In the narrow room,
I unroll the raffia mat.
How long
did I stare
at the grey ceiling
before sleep
came? Somewhere
between the darkest
hour &
the darkest hour,
he wakes me.
In steel silence,
I see his hand—
no, it is the gnarled
koboko.

Hollow

In this room, a TV sits on a desk. I look from its apathy to the sky
-blue cap of what is between my fingers. Tip unpacks. My tongue knows
the *Asiento de Negros* gave Britain complete
liberty to feed Spanish colonies with four thousand
eight hundred enslaved Africans every year for thirty years.
What did the ocean say the first time it saw manacles on a child?

No language. The child
with smoky quartz eyes, sky
sagging, deflates on the edge of prowling years.
The mouth of a musket knows
a bight where a thousand-
slitted bones flounder. In ruin, what stands complete?

The room heaves. A complete
bipartite graph, I connect to displacement—child
clamped to dark. The thousand-
th decimal place grief perforates on my body like a sky
of bruises. Anyone who has done the math knows
the ocean is an electric chair. What did the years

in the years
& after the years not take? Ships at a complete
angle. I take it: everything the road knows—
swollen wrists of child-
ren. Their heads shaved with blunt knives. Oiled. Seared. Sold & resold under a
different sky.
Fathers tacked beneath decks. Fetid air. Months. Same position. Months. Perhaps
three thousand

feet above sea level this poem looks like a flailing song. Give me two thousand
reasons why a poem is not a wound. This year's
splinter—Ralph Yarl shot in the head for knocking on the wrong door. A sky-
lark is shrilling & I'm breaking into incomplete
shadows behind my ink. Outside the child-
ish spring is on the arms of saucer magnolias. Forgive me—who knows?

—I don't know what the mother who fights back with a hunger strike knows.
Only something fierce against flesh—as in a thousand
scourges—until splatter after quick splatter. O child-
hood—years
from now, what will grow inside this poem? Doesn't desolation come complete
with an undertaker sky?

The throb & what it knows through a sky-
less day. On the face of the child born in burning years
—a thousand-yard stare. This ash. Ash. Cold complete.

Roots

The griot taking me
around Salaga knows
the heavy frame set
called memory.
We have been to the old
dry wells, to the mass
grave site, which is not
too far from
where the hyenas scavenged.
What did
I expect to find here, days
on the road from Elmina,
disappearing anthill after mound
of disappearing anthill,
with the Castle's anguish
still scything,
except further hollowness.
Across from where we are
standing, a little boy
is running after a little boy
flying a kite.
There is the faint voice of someone
singing in Hausa in the distance.
"A baobab
once stood here..." he is saying to me,
forefinger pointing.
We are standing
on the very ground for centuries
they were bartered.
Our feet red
dust.

Passing

I am passing the poem to this city
& its watermarks of loneliness.

For every poem, there is a poem
with a coin in its mouth.

It is that month again.
Sometimes my footsteps frighten the raccoons
when I walk by the dumpster. Sometimes
they stand for a moment, charred
eyes gleaming, before rummaging resumes.

I am passing the poem to aunties who pray
for hours, food getting cold, & uncles who chew obnoxiously.
I am passing the poem to green gods. Maple. Honey locust.
Sycamore, black walnut, hackberry. Zigzag
twigs that touch foreground
of sadness. My sadness.

The rabbits here are built like 40-year-old toddlers.
Sometimes all I want to do is sit & pet them.
Something about wild roses along old footpaths, still air against dusky skin—
waking to the TV's blank face, to rain in the middle of the night this time of year.

I am not passing the poem to the hole that is always my account balance, nor Hinge girl
who says her most irrational fear is people from third-world countries.

There is a lake beyond that field where little girls play
soccer on Friday evenings, where bluegills bubble
up in innocence, eager mouths for what my hands hold.
Some days I come face to face with deer, almost aware
of what binds us in thin woods.

I am passing the poem to my father. Sitting outside his own house.
Loose white singlet. A glass of ogogoro in one hand.
Listening to Osadebe. Watching the evening sky.
Two weeks before the accident.
Two weeks before the accident.
Two.

Late Spring

The chiaroscuro
of tulip poplars.
The scarlet tanager is back
from its travel along the long white
dress of the border.
Someone once told me I hide
my sadness well
behind all the birds
in my poems.
A slap of wind pushes us to go,
then to go.
You turn by a boulder to kiss the cold
tip of my nose. I will keep an eye
out for wonder.

Greyhound from the State with More Pigs Than People

Less than fifteen
minutes in, the big fella
on the aisle seat is already asleep,
squashing me in. Two rows up,
the tall man wearing a red
baseball hat eats a burrito.
Doesn't the stench from the restroom
make him want to vomit?
I try working the Rubik's cube
but the man behind is on the phone
complaining about some guy
named Joseph, *a goofy-ass piece of shit*,
who has refused to pay him back his money.
He is a bish. I'm telling you that he is a bish!
he yells again and again.
Outside, vast green. Deere
tractors stock-still in cornfields.
Am I not what is always moving?
Water child, what is my life
within my life? Someone's carry-on baggage
clatters down from one of the storage
compartments, nearly hitting the woman with child.
At the Speedway convenience store,
the driver brings the motorcoach
to a stop. *Our ride is long*, he says,
so use this opportunity to stretch your legs.
And if you're planning on stealing
anything from the store, please let me know
so I can taze and take your ass to jail.
We laugh. Big fella only changes
his snoring gear.

Ember

"Dear Mama, George Hanger has sent me a black boy eleven years old and very honest, but the Duke don't like me having a black... if you like him instead of Michel I will send him, he will be a cheap servant and you will make a Christian of him and a good boy; if you don't like him they say Lady Rockingham wants one."

—Duchess of Devonshire to her mother, circa 1790, National Museums Liverpool

Ọmọ Ìyá mi, I am writing from inside the year a police officer crushed a brother's song with his knee. Somewhere right now, a baton is coming down on a head, bodies are being teargassed and slammed against concrete. What is a poem before the hunger of a bullet? Just now, a firefinch on a branch. I am thinking about you. Again. Today, I want to show you something simple, like how to make a paper boat. Or the rabbits in the backyard: how they forage in morning light, then huddle together like men discussing the details of a coup. Beloved, while the sun pelts this town's dusty roofs, we will ride our bicycles down the street and buy ice cream from the old Igbo man with a straw hat. Because I don't like the vanilla flavour, I will have the vanilla flavour. Perhaps you will have the chocolate. While we eat, I will tell you about the day the crazy neighbourhood dog chased me and how I abandoned my water bucket and ran the way a man does when he hears the last bus is about to leave the station. You will sprout into laughter, and I will watch you, your warm full life

Look

The trees stand the way trees stand.
Six squirrels climb up one & take positions.
The one with a slightly darker tail scratches
the upper part of its body
with hind claws. The rest inspect the air.
Nothing bothers them.
Not the cold. Not the bald eagles from Wisconsin
who ride along the River
searching for a fresh meal.
I have been told
never to write about this city,
but what about these small, steadfast workers
carrying their good life
from white branch to branch?
How many people, the poems
not quite coming,
have sat on this chestnut chair & watched
these forest caretakers play
hide & seek?
A pen drops
on the floor. I shift
as the professor leans to adjust
the mic. From the back
of the room, someone surrenders
a question I know
but don't understand.

There Is This

Inside Elmina Castle, the Dutch
church, hulking, sprawls above
a part of the female dungeons.
I enter the way one enters an unwashed wound.
From the window, the ocean's
green, funereal green. What I know punches
through—bodies under in the backbreaking heat.
Shackles grating bones. Whip hooks—a mother's blood-matted
back. The reek of what is dank so strong it is strong.
Teen, heart thumping, about to be uprooted
for the governor's bed.

These folks said *amen*.

(S)hell

Every year
the harvest is the same hollow song.
The photos rankle—
Farm after cassava
farm murky. With crude oil
spills. New shoots suffocate
in clods. Not spared, the river
looks like a warzone.

Somewhere a child is trekking to school with a growling stomach.

I push the laptop aside and stand by
the window. There are no birds
on the guava tree this morning.
Already the harmattan is running through
the town. Already it is November.
Didn't the land wail the day they hung the Ogoni 9?
As a kid I always carried old newspapers in my bag—not for words
but photos. Even then, something about Sani Abacha's
face reminded me of gravediggers' hoes.
And hasn't every barrel
since '58 etched our names on a tombstone?

I return to my desk, to black keys & screen,
to mullet bloating among reeds,
to startled field mouse, the half-mast face
of the mangrove forest. To silence, always
the broken clock on the wall, stiff & ashen.

In October

depressed & not
taking your ART, your
CD4 count drops.
Night sweats. The ache
& then the ache. That rash.
Today your mother
sits on the plastic chair in
the small white room.
Today she looks out
the window. Today she flips
through the old
photo album with blistered
fingers that toil
on other people's cassava farms.
Today she watches your frail
sleeping body.
She knows what the neighbours
say behind closed doors.
How they warn their children to stay
away from you, pulling
them by the ear
with lectures about
your supposed whoredom.
How they call this *thing* eating
your system
your punishment.
How they look
at you like rodent shit
on the street.
It is the year
before the year
of masks.

It is the rainy season
& some bird always cries
from outside
cold.

The Tree of Forgetfulness

> "They were made to walk around a supposedly magical tree called the Tree of Forgetfulness. Men had to go round it nine times, women and children seven. This experience, they were told, would make them forget everything - their names, their family, and the life they had once had."
>
> —*BBC News*

You are only a kid
but know nothing can disarrange the fabric of blood
—your little sister, head thrown back,
how easily she laughs
when you unroll tales of Ìjàpá.
Your mother tongue is a window. Elders, under harvest
moon, their hands on ancestral drums.
Even now the egúngún still sways
in your heart.

On this road, trodding towards
what falls towards dust,
skin raw-stinging
from mosquitoes, you pray the boy with
vertical tribal marks
on his right cheek—the boy who asked for water,
who begged for water
& was given the back
of a musket—gets up.
But you understand silence,
how it clatters. & clatters.

Someone's father is lifting
a song. Along night edges,
some nocturnal call,
song with no song. A dungeon is a skull
before anything else. Dawn

clenches, & you're carrying
through the ashen door, carrying whole
across ocean. You know
before voodoo there was memory.

The Year After the Year After the Year My Father Died

I make plans with people &
pray they cancel.

In my recurring dream, you're the one
driving but it's me who is tired.
You bring the grey
car to a stop & we drink from cold
bottles of Limca.
Moon looming, I want
to say something
then I wake to ceiling
fan squeak.

My father, I now live in a city
far from the village
you grew up in, that quiet
village where old men burn
their hair after barbering.

Fall is here.
The sidewalk crunches
with couples walking
their dogs.
On the white
porch I take the poem
apart again.

Thorn

My last night in Cape Coast & sleep
will not come. I turn this way & that
until finally I get up from bed, slip
into flip-flops, & walk down Awonakofua street.
The moon plodders
in the starless sky. Two stray cats gangle
under the chalky glow
of the streetlight not too far from the cobbler shop.
At Absa Bank, I turn left. Then,
right into the street where I helped
an old man unload his cart of mangoes last week.
I walk until Cape Coast Castle blanches
into view. My smoky
ink flumps here. Centuries
later, their ghosts are still writhing—
kids wrenched from coastal
villages, mother & mother
of the mother, man who promised
his children a new tale about the bat-eared fox.
In the empty street, only the wailing
of the ocean, wave after wave, obsidian.

Understory

He wakes me before 6— few taps
on the shoulder followed by *a man*
cannot afford to be a deep sleeper.
Foggy, I stagger
through the doorway.

For breakfast, we have
the warmth of our boots.

            Close, but not too close,
a water chevrotain takes
notes between two rubber trees.
Smooth reddish-brown coat. Eyes this

large. Are we on holy ground
& don't know?
Did it bow to something bigger than our lives
as it turns away in the rainforest?

Three days ago, he had placed
the traps woven by his weathered hands,
palm fruit lures inside, at every mouth
of the sweeping pond. Now as he bends

to lift the first trap
heavy with crabs, snakeheads,
& eels, I watch him with understanding.

Here & here. Ọsẹ, under
a palette of fresh faith, you made me
a bamboo flute. I still sing.

Object Permeance

Creak. Cobwebs.
A halo of dust. Two
petite chairs, back
to back
but not touching.
The boombox looks
like a girl thrown into
an arranged marriage.

Singed

air. Nearby the rabbits have taken over
that truck you were against buying.
I imagine they throw little furry parties
inside it, dancing to beauty
at dusk. The creek

at the back is swelling.
The questions are growing new heads

through the crack
of the day
& I'm watching
a singing bird watch
the cashew tree
no one
believed in
sag with fruit.

The Atlantic

Every day in Elmina, gold town,
here where almost every canoe
bears a name that serenades God, here
where December
heat roasts scalps, I stand before you.
Who doesn't know you don't
have Alzheimer's or that the past
still flounders
on your cold endlessness?
I look through you and looking I don't
want to look at you.
Like the titan you are named after
you begin with fire
and live in heaviness.
I don't have to think
Portuguese or Dutch ships, their grey
hunger taking & taking,
or what the atomic
eyes of these pied crows have seen
or even the Castle's bleached walls
which always remind me of bones
to know you are everything
returning
with no tongue.

In Lieu of a Title

My mother has turned the room
where I wet my bed until I clocked fourteen
into a storeroom—old fishing
rods, umbrellas,
buckets, garri sacks on wooden slabs.
I stand by the window.

Across the street, two girls
stand facing each other
playing *Tinko*.
Palm against palm, back of hand
quick against back
of hand, they are singing:
Tinko Tinko
Tikonko Tinko
Tinko Tinko
Tikonko Tinko.
Girl with red ribbons in blackberry
hair wins. They start again,
their laughter trickling

towards me. I chuckle.
Just then
our neighbour steps
outside with a transistor
radio playing that type
of song that makes you
miss home.

Port Harcourt

> *"Doctors in Rivers State have been sounding the alarm in recent years over the mounting medical toll of soot and air pollution on millions of people in cities across the oil producing Niger Delta region..."*
>
> —*The Guardian*

Another year, another
year of the soot. Killer
whale-black, it tyrants
in our prams, broth
bowls, streets, lungs. Every day
I watch my neighbour watch
the sky. What stands between us stands
between us with no song. Last week
in someone else's backyard
sparrows tumbled down
swollen with acid
rain. Everywhere I go
the tiny coffins of their eyes chafe
against my heart. O Garden City, O
garden withering. Somewhere
mounds of tyres are burning. Somewhere
along creeks, among blackened
forest trees, more drums are heating
& thick dark is smothering
& smothering. Mask
or no mask, someone
is always coughing. At the market
where men are better hagglers
even the mangoes
are almost the colour of polished basalt
eggs. I look away, O
city of my true love, home

of the choicest *bole*, O
I look away
to a beggar on
the sidewalk, his head
bowed like a tortured
prayer

Potluck

Blue sky, mango trees
festooned with nests of village weavers.
Neruda, smiling and wearing
a shirt almost too warm
for the weather, is the last to arrive.
I take the gourd of palmwine and the square
container filled with Nkwobi from him.
Oliver is playing Schoenberg on the piano.
Awoonor watches, surrenders
to virtuosic fingers, and starts swaying.
The sight of music going through a man
is the beginning of light.
Someone has set the table.
Tangy glazed meatballs.
Vegan coleslaw. Peach sangria.
There is kolanut. Which means there is life.
What has poetry taught you? Brooks asks me.
When in doubt, choose rebellion, I answer.
She laughs then nods.
Later in a game of spoons
someone other than Awoonor wins.
For dessert, Achebe tells
us a story so flawless, so Achebe.
Call it a river nun's touch.
Call it the pulse between worlds.
Listening to them talk and laugh at each
other's jokes, these plainspoken folk,
I am not thinking of endings.

The Door of No Return in Elmina Castle

It begins
with silence,
like strangled
syntax. It
begins with
silence, then
it begins.
From the murk
of dungeons
to murk.
Everything
still cold.
These manacles,
stark white
of bone.
This mother,
to fit through,
starved for weeks.
This kid's wide
pupils as coarse
hands drag
him through
like a
hearse.

Beneath Silence

Begin with carps, bonga shads,
long-neck croakers & banded lampeyes
—all ghosts
with rotting opercula—
lying on the dingy tongue of the river
like mannequins.
The moon eyes
away from the crude
oil company
while greasy
bones of mangroves convulse
in their sleep.

Look! the antelope passes without stopping.
Then the swamp
nightjar. Then the stranger.

Why have I brought you here?
Why do I still bring you here?

Something whole, pellucid
like the glass sponge in the northwestern Gulf,
lived here. At this bank
I washed my mother's freshly peeled cassava.
Fathers cast
nets & caught joy. They turned this way
& that way
giving thanks to aqua nuns.
Wet shoes in hand, you see what the future holds
by how a bulrush sways. You could taste
the air, wingful & unflinching.

Because in ruin
only ruin,
I must carry the poem this way
far to the middle
where a canoe, stuck, waits.

This

Facing each other,
nearly full after a hot meal
of eba & Banga soup,
my mother & I talk about everything. Climbing
price of beef. The former village
drunk who now throws parties for stray dogs.
The bird building a nest
on the orange tree by my father's grave.
Pale-almond beak, but I have never seen
its kind around here, she says.
To bring the subject of marriage closer
again, she goes: so & so
from your age group is expecting
another baby. & so & so
parents are meeting next week
to discuss the items on the bridal list.
I throw a smile.
Outside night stands against the window
like an armourbearer.
My mother heads for the kitchen.

You wouldn't like me as a child.
I used to steal things
& swiftly discard the urge
to return them—mangoes,
the neighbour's coins, banana-flavoured
chewing gum. What has changed
in this room? The crispy scent still rises to greet.
Someone has taken the TV.
Do they know it requires a few slaps
on the sides for it to work?
From a brioche-coloured bottle,

I pour kerosene into the lantern
& wait for the wick to drink.
She comes back with a tray of roasted
groundnuts. Between cracked
hulls, laughter.
Dawn, before I leave for the airport,
my mother assembles three songs across
my right shoulder. You are planted,
she says, flourish.

Down Up

stab.
for loved ones
of children wailing
in his ears, the voices
but whenever he stops to lie down,
Francisco is weary
& smells like trash truck juice.
His beard is overgrown
singing when they see him coming.
Even the birds cease
like that. No one looks his way.
like this. He roams
barefoot. He roams
& he roams
Francisco Félix de Sousa is homeless
In the afterlife.

In

Cancún, I am friends with the stray
brown dog who lives between this side of town
and that other with gold ring fingers.
When I arrived at the Airbnb he ran to me,
tail-wagging, sniffing
as if he knew I had come from the cold
chamber of loneliness. I call him Nico.

Today the sky looks like the aquamarine
necklace of a rich auntie
with no kids. We are walking past schoolchildren
in white and blood orange uniforms, past ice
cream men with little carts, shoeshiners
whose only language is hard
work, and the map takes us to the wrong location.
Tired, and because Parque
Ecológica Ombligo Verde is the closest
green, we enter
to Iguanas sunbathing.
Here, trees pulsing with Inca doves,
I am suddenly thinking childhood, my childhood—
pouring rain days. How I would drop paper boats
into small waterfall on the side of the road
and run after them laughing.
Nico wakes and we share two apples. I read
Mervyn Morris to him. Then
a little Edward Baugh.

On our way back, inside the Combi, I listen as
the girl who tried
to pet Nico when we got in tells her friend
that owning just one guinea pig

in Switzerland is illegal
because they get so lonely.
Thereafter silence gnaws at our feet.

Tonight under streetlamps,
I am playing street football
with the neighbourhood kids.
I turn to see if Nico is watching
from the old couch under the almond tree
but he is gone. From one of the balconies,
a woman's singing voice, maracas.

Winter in Iowa City

Is embarrassing.
My eyes water profusely
whenever I walk in the cold, crispy air.
Going up East Washington
to see my friend
whose apartment is a failed
attempt at a movie set, a woman
walks up to me smiling & says, "It's okay, everything
will be alright" & offers a Kleenex.
I want to tell her it is only a natural response, this
thing with my eyes. Does it matter?
I thank her.
Years from now I will remember
the light from her eyes
still warms this page.

Collocation

In the grand canyon of things, have I been calling
to dry sprigs, descending into sediment
like infauna? Late at night making love, peignoir
& a glaciated window, you touched me everywhere
but here. What is warmth if it comes from under
neath the wooden toolshed of your life as claw
hammer. The wind bristles with rye
grass & across the cistern of memory, the rib
cage knows what murks. Moths against head
lights. Silence, too, can be rinsed even though it is skin
less. The air. The air. Always the air
for the siloed day opening in a field. In the rear
view mirror, only the flat & wobbly plank sign that reads
hitchhikers may be escaping inmates.

Delisted

Something is always losing its face.
I will wear only sackcloth, little brother Kaua'i 'ō'ō.
A forest bleeds in my throat.
& now a metal door slammed against your soft *Oo'oo—oo-auh.*
When I am not kneeling, I will be kneeling,
face to floating river of candles, Maui nukupu'u.
Even now, in the distance, dark
like dark. I will not sweep my house, Kauai akialoa.
Large Kauai thrush in the moist gulch of my eye, I will not bathe.
For you, Little Mariana fruit bat, my head will be shaved.
& there will be ash on my head, Flat pigtoe, Scioto madtom
ash between my fingers, San Marcos gambusia, Po`ouli.
Ash raw around my ankles,
ash ash Southern acornshell Upland combshell,
Stirrupshell, ash ash ash ash Green-blossom pearly mussel,
Yellow-blossom pearly mussel,
Turgid-blossom pearly mussel, Tubercled-blossom pearly mussel,
ash Molokai creeper ash ash Kauai nukupuu,
Bachman's warbler ash ash Bridled white-eye.
Maui ākepa, dusty green sister,
I will not wear any jewellery.

The Volta

for Kofi Awoonor

Early December in Ìbàdàn.
The harmattan is out.
In the chapped back of the classroom,
dark brown sandals, almost twenty &
still in secondary school,
I listen as our teacher anoints
again with your lines.
These lines. O how they touch the burnt
end of my life.

It rains on one side of the street
morning the news barrels into me.

Why didn't I ever write you a letter?
How in every crowd
there is always a song. You.
Son of Wheta, you whose light, even in solitary
confinement, roared against
the dark of those khaki sharks.

Now I am watching the flame
lilies. Flipping through pages of fog
to this place where your baobab
body falls to a fusillade
of red-winged birds. Now only the silence
follows me around, follows
me around with its cast-iron

face. September. September & its sky gall—

Honey

Honey, your eyes, especially
your eyes—small dark opals
I cannot resist.

Night knows the secret behind your hidden ears
& such knowledge drinks from this
crusty land you reign. Skin tough like loneliness,

what warm tunnel
did you rise from this morning?
I have watched you dismantle a king

cobra, claw after grisly claw,
invade beehives with fart chemical.

Everyone wants you to be kind
as if kindness isn't the most boring thing in the wild.

Blessed are the mean.

Still

Say leopard orchids /angels /unreported /deforested /dreams /missing breasts /dusk /discovered /strangled hibiscus /say for every dead girl, there is your country, which means a man's sledgehammer-hand. Who among them doesn't look like you. Who among them isn't. In the house of your desires, there are dry leaves, red-beaked birds scooping out light. Who knows what it's like for a mother to pull her baby from a pool of blood, to look without looking at the empty chair at dinner. To love is to be against forgetting. Once, a man you loved called love a wild thing that must be domesticated. You're thinking again about that dry season you spent with him in a city whose name gleams like a razor, razor to your jugular vein. Here, between dislocation & some hollowed shadow, //hear Iniobong Umoren //hear Uwaila Omozuwa //hear Barakat Bello //hear Joy Onoh /here Favour Okechukwu //here Comfort Benjamin //here Cynthia Okogosu. No baobabs tonight. No. No salted water. You're writing with the silence after the body is on the ground, after everyone moves on in a country that lists you as inventory alongside exit wounds &
coffins.

Sunday

after reading Robert Hayden's "Those Winter Sundays"

Sunday my mother wakes us up, and we go to church.
Sunday my father wakes up, washes his car, and
goes back to sleep.
When his friends visit in the evening, I am the one
who serves the ogogoro and breaks the kolanut.
Then I sit in a corner and watch
them, farmers and fishermen whose bodies
know the furnace that is the sun, pour libation.
They talk about the fishing season. The declining
population of snakeheads. They talk about the clan
and who has another concubine.
The light in their eyes droops
when one mentions that almost half the rainforest
has fallen to government bulldozers.
There is silence. I refill their glasses.
One

night after one such visit,
I take the bottle of ogogoro and sit outside the house—
that is the last thing I remember. Next, it is dawn,
and I am lying on the path that leads to the pit latrine,
black fat flies buzzing over me. I stand up, mouth
still reeking, and stagger to the front
of the house, where my parents are sitting.
One look at me, and my father
doubles up with laughter.
My mother shakes her head
and says to me, *you have allowed the devil*
to use your head for a drum.

I Wakeful

on moonless roads what am I praying for
hands cupped around a rainstorm
I have seen how the grave tracks my thirst
still like a mugger crocodile
the machinery just the machinery
& where it comes down on everything
again & again with burnt syllables
impossible syntax staring down
your face behind redwood behind white stinkwood
behind mountain cliff behind swallows
I want to stand in the inner yard of this crack
where your laughter simmers
such waiting awaits torn hymnals & heavy
branches no light unspooling shadows
this dusty staccato
that ice cream before the last ice cream
eaten on a wooden bench
because time is saltier than memory
because the two live beneath each other
& promise &

Passage

Corrugated-iron sky.
Coffee with another friend who drags
along the weight of his student loans.
Some poets talk about their grandmas
but do not write about them.
Mine died when I was in Ìbàdàn.
That was the year I said grief is one long ad you cannot skip.
Some days all I think about is her hands.
Hands that showed me how to hold
a hoe & be tender around every stalk of corn.
Hands that hid the earthenware
of my body from the occasional thunder
of that house. That bought my one good Okrika sweater.
Weeks after the funeral, her pied cats, hyphenated
by absence, leaned to absence.
Can you build a grieving
centre inside a poem?
Some nights all I have is the social holiness of metaphors.
Girl from New York (or is it Texas?) whose answer to almost every
question is *I am from New York, baby*. Skim milk. February.
Caked boots. Clementines. Shelf panting with banned books.
The last essay says to avoid metaphors. The essay
is void. Poets war. Didn't Okigbo leave Ìbàdàn for the war.
Town-crier, I still breathe your dark green words. Somewhere
right now it is summer & an ice cream truck is gathering
neighbourhood children. Here the body knows
but not enough about what grows against window panes.
Across the street, only a man's neck, only snow
underneath tyres. Let what kisses bloodroot
kiss snow trillium by rue anemone. The way a home holds
long. Let silence cave. Further, & in the description below, let this be
the polonaise set to a triple meter of lights.

200–300

That's the number
of Cross
River gorillas left.
Every morning,
just before sunrise,
I sit at the window
a man not ready
open for what
the day
holds. I don't know
what it is like
to always be
on the run, to have
your bones picked
clean, or the language
of the forest
after an infantry
of chainsaws
walks through it.
What I know comes
in palpable
fragments.
Their dark
caramel eyes,
the tired
little ones
asleep on chests
of mothers.
How softly
their hands
will open
into mine
like a daisy.

This is Not the Title

Razors & syringes scare me.
Doctors, too—one, I can't stand
the smell of their office, and two,
the only doktor in our village looks like a mammoth—
so I've been hiding it for weeks.

My best friend Kome says to use palm oil
since I got it from pointing my finger at the moon.
"Don't point your finger at the moon!"
I have applied palm oil, but the pain pummels.
And yesterday, at the birthday party of a woman we don't know,
while we ate like men with health insurance,
Karo, our new friend from down the street, said palm oil alone
would not get the job done. "Put some poop
and piss on it. Your poop and piss,
not someone else's," he added. I almost threw up.
This same Karo was the one who told us that
a sunshower meant a lioness was giving birth.
Where does his ten-year-old brain get these ideas
from? I murmur inaudibly to myself
as I rub my poop and piss on
it before tying a piece of cloth around
it in the thatched latrine.

Night
and my agony is like the sting of broken clavicles. I writhe
on the raffia mat. I can hear my father talking
with my mother in the parlour.
I pretend everything is fine when he calls me
to bring him a toothpick. I offer him the toothpick
with my *left* hand. Ọsẹ, ẹva dhọ whẹ hẹ,
I say quickly to him, but his mild annoyance

has turned to something else—the face people
make when they whiff what stinks.
"Let me see your right hand." My father is not
the type of man who likes repeating himself.
Slowly he unwraps the tawny cloth, and there,
on the corner of my forefinger,
fat with pus, it throbs.
My mother gasps, places her palms on her head,
and exclaims, "Oghene!"
"Go heat me some water," my father gruffs.
She heads for the kitchen.
"Let me grab my box," he says to himself,
already walking towards his bedroom.
I know one of the things he keeps inside
that wooden box. Outside the bald moon
grazes the window.

i hold the earth at night in a field

in another version of the poem
i am on his rickety bicycle, clutching
my slate, the dread of that building
called school
crust-hard in my throat
& he is saying *omo mẹ, be better*
than me.

in the version before that other version,
he is brushing his teeth with a neem
stick in the harmattan dawn.

in the version before this version
a blackbird
smelling of deforestation
sits on a windowsill &

i am pulling parts of
him from the roots of a river,
a shared orange, a song
& calling the space in my throat a working object
that breaks down that remembers that breaks down.

in this version, in the open coffin,
he looks like a boy asleep in a hurricane.

Envoi

after a line from César Vallejo's "Black Stone on a White Stone"

As I was saying,
what was I saying,
yes, as I was saying
there is only one way
to say this: I will die in Ìbàdàn.
It will not happen
during the month wild
hibiscus feral.
I will have on the watch the woman I love
but did not marry
gifted me before taking the night
train. All the poems I did not write will
protest for themselves
against themselves
in white desolation.
I try to write the dark. Clean-shaven like jazz?
I swear. I try.
I have eaten Amala Skye. If that isn't paradise, I don't
know what is.
Before saying a few words at the funeral,
someone who looks like a character from Papa Ajasco
will read a poem I don't like. It is okay. It is my funeral.
As I was saying, whoever,
please remember my cat, tar-black—
she will again be in one of the rooms
trying to hide my ankle socks.

Acknowledgments

My sincere gratitude to the editors of the following publications, where these poems first appeared or are forthcoming, sometimes in altered versions:

Academy of American Poets' Poets.org: "200-300"
Efiko Magazine: "Collocation"
The Hudson Review: "Understory," "This"
The Kenyon Review: "Grit"
Mineral Lit Mag: "i hold the earth at night in a field"
Ploughshares: "Waiting"
Poetry Ireland Review: "Potluck," "Late Spring"
POETRY Magazine: "Mass," "The Year My Father Died"
The Poetry Review (UK): "Object Permeance"
Quarterly West: "Passing"

I would like to thank the Stanley-University of Iowa Foundation Support Organization for awarding me a Stanley Award for International Research, which enabled my research at the slave castles in Ghana and made some of the poems in this book possible. I also want to thank Diane Seuss for believing in these poems. Thanks also to J, Charlie, Chance, and all the wonderful people at TRP. I sincerely thank my professors at the Iowa Writers' Workshop: Tracie Morris, Mark Levine, James Gavin, and Shane Book. I would also like to express my gratitude to the following people for the community they provide: Amiya Moretta, Jeremy Karn, Sergio Rios, Xiadi Zhai, 'Gbenga Adeoba, Otosirieze Obi-Young, Adedayo Agarau, Constant Williams, Prince Bush, Reyumeh Ejue, Helynna Lin, Terri Draper, William Okwan, Pamilerin Jacob, Aiwanose Odafen, Owolabi Onamade, Godwin Henry, Daniel Ochekwu, IJ, Niyi Ademoroti, Adams Adeosun, Obasiota Ibe, SP, Joshua Ikechukwu, Aaron Faronbi, Soji Cole, Audrey Obuobisa-Darko, James Braun, Romeo Oriogun, Rabiu Mamman, Mame Oba, Okwudili Nebeolisa, and Mofiyinfoluwa Okupe. I beg forgiveness from anyone I may have missed.

Finally, I would like to thank my family, especially Benni and my Mama, for the light that is their prayer.

Acknowledgments

About the Author

OTHUKE UMUKORO, Nigerian poet and playwright, is a graduate of the Iowa Writers' Workshop, where he won the Academy of American Poets University Poetry Prize. Winner of the prestigious Brunel International African Poetry Prize, his work appears in *Ploughshares*, *POETRY*, *The Hudson Review*, *The Poetry Review* (UK), *Poetry Ireland Review*, and elsewhere.

Winner of The 2024 X. J. Kennedy Poetry Prize

Selected by Diane Seuss

Established in 1998, The X. J. Kennedy Prize highlights one book per year for excellence in a full-length poetry collection.

Previous Winners:
2023—Rob Carney—*The Book of Drought*
2022—Sebastian Merrill—*GHOST :: SEEDS*
2021—Kathleen Rooney—*Where Are the Snows*
2020—Brooke Sahni—*Before I Had the Word*
2019—Caroline M. Mar—*Special Education*
2018—Garret Keizer—*The World Pushes Back*
2017—Jay Udall—*Because a Fire in Our Heads*
2016—Jeff Hardin—*No Other Kind of World*
2015—Gwen Hart—*The Empress of Kisses*
2014—Corinna McClanahan Schroeder—*Inked*
2013—Ashley Mace Havird—*The Garden of the Fugitives*
2012—Jeff Worley—*A Little Luck*
2011—James McKean—*We Are the Bus*
2010—George Drew—*The View from Jackass Hill*
2009—Joshua Coben—*Maker of Shadows*
2008—Ashley Renee—*Basic Heart*
2007—William Baer—*"Bocage" and Other Sonnets*
2006—Becky Gould Gibson, *Aphrodite's Daughter*
2005—Deborah Bogen—*Landscape with Silos*
2004—Lee Rudolph—*A Woman and a Man, Ice-Fishing*
2003—Eric Nelson—*Terrestrials*
2002—Jan Lee Ande—*Reliquary*
2001—Jorn Ake—*Asleep in the Lightning Fields*
2000—Barbara Lau—*The Long Surprise*
1999—Philip Heldrich—*Good Friday*
1998—Gray Jacobik—*The Surface of Last Scattering*